This bite-sized boo[k]
useful overview of
and will help you t[o]

- Prepare well for [...]
- Enhance your inte[r]personal skills
- Deal better with conflict situations
- Provide constructive feedback
- Confidently manage important conversations

> In conversation, we practice good human behaviours. We become visible to one another. We gain insights and new understandings
>
> Margaret Wheatley

The power of conversations

Conversations hold immense power and can enhance our lives in so many different ways. Conversations help us to form new connections and strengthen existing ones. We can learn so much through conversation because it can help us to make sense of something we don't understand and provide us with the opportunity to explore different perspectives. Conversations can also help us to solve problems and unleash our creativity.

Conversation is the life-blood of our relationships and helps us to bond with others. It is also necessary for effective communication because when we don't talk about something we may ruminate or speculate which can cause unnecessary anxiety. It's good to talk.

> What mental health needs is more sunlight, more candour, and more unashamed conversation
>
> Glenn Close

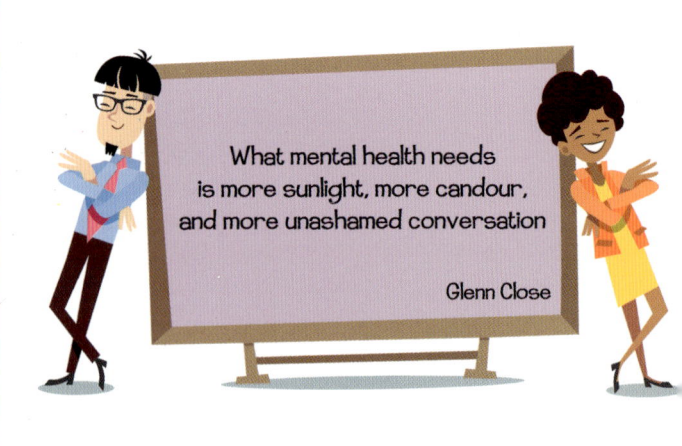

Conversation and wellbeing

Conversations are the gateway to learning about ourselves and other people. Talking about feelings and thoughts can help boost our confidence, reduce stress and positively impact on our overall wellbeing.

Our conversation style, both with other people and with ourselves, can have a big impact on our mental health. By improving our ability to communicate and comfortably articulate how we feel will help us to build confidence when dealing with more challenging conversations. It is helpful to manage our stress levels and approach conversations in a calmer and more emotionally intelligent way.

A real conversation always contains an invitation. You are inviting another person to reveal themselves to you, to tell you who they are or what they want

David Whyte

Be a skilled conversationalist

Being a skilled conversationalist is about keeping the energy of a conversation flowing. It is about being able to articulate ourselves well whilst actively listening to what the other person has to say too.

This is important in terms of building positive relationships with other people both professionally and personally. Being able to speak to people with interest, ease and confidence will help conversations flow more easily and help us establish stronger connections. Being a skilled conversationalist will also help us to be more self-assured and prepared in any work or social situation.

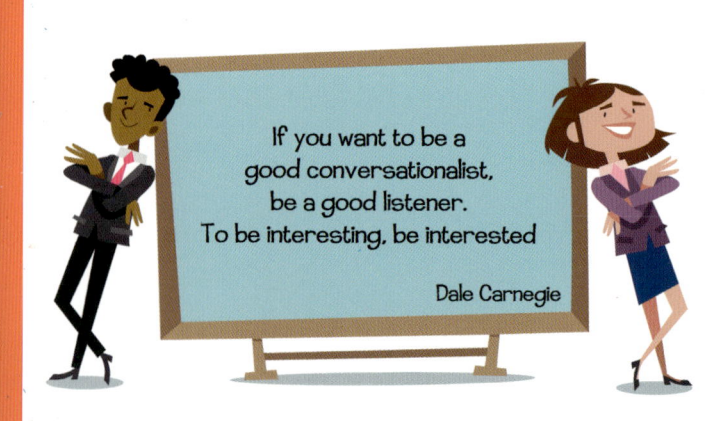

> If you want to be a good conversationalist, be a good listener. To be interesting, be interested
>
> Dale Carnegie

Embrace conversations

One sure way to embrace and enjoy conversations is to find everyone we meet interesting. Human beings are fascinating and everyone we meet has a story to tell and knows something we don't. Listening to other people's stories is a great way to be more inclusive and broaden our own perspective.

Conversation can also provide social support and help people to feel more involved and less lonely. Striking up a conversation with someone new can lead to all sorts of unknown opportunities and interesting discoveries. It can also help us to become a more practised conversationalist and each conversation we have is a mini adventure.

START A CONVERSATION with someone new

> There is no conversation more boring than the one where everybody agrees
>
> Michel de Montaigne

Handling challenging conversations

Sometimes making conversations can be challenging, especially if we don't know someone very well or we lack confidence in certain situations. Tackling sensitive issues can be tricky especially if we anticipate that the other person may get defensive about whatever it is we want or need to talk about.

While it is tempting to avoid these kinds of conversations, doing so could potentially lead to resentment, stress and even become harder to resolve at a later stage. Addressing challenging conversations skilfully can help strengthen relationships and create better understanding. We won't always agree with what other people have to say. However, the variety of viewpoints can be the spice in the conversation and add a bit more flavour!

> Psychological safety is a belief that one will not be punished or humiliated for speaking up with ideas, questions, concerns or mistakes
>
> Amy Edmonson

Psychological safety

Psychological safety is the belief that we won't be punished or humiliated for speaking up and is a fundamental ingredient if we want to have open, healthy and honest conversations. Psychological safety means that we trust the person we are talking to and feel confident that they won't embarrass, reject or punish us for sharing our honest thoughts and feelings and admitting our vulnerabilities.

Trust and respect is the foundation upon which psychological safety is built. Building trust, however, takes patience and commitment. In order to build trust, we need to be patient and take small steps in each relationship we have. It takes courage to build trust and it also takes time.

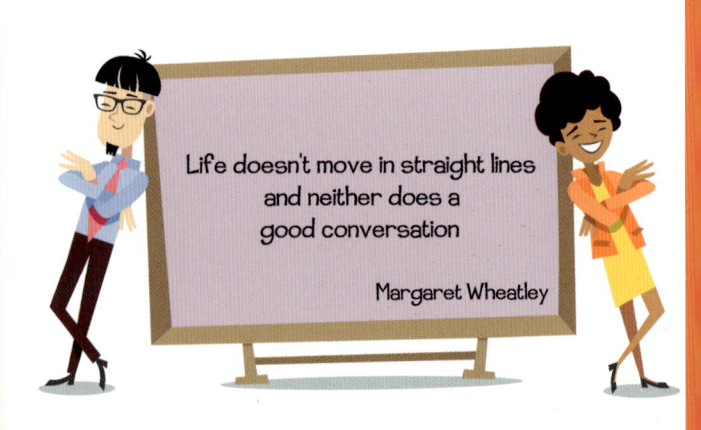

Life doesn't move in straight lines
and neither does a
good conversation

Margaret Wheatley

How to have great conversations

The foundation for a great conversation requires a good set of communication skills and it is about having a dialogue not a monologue. Ultimately it is about balancing our ability to speak and listen.

There are many ways that we can have honest, healthy and fulfilling conversations and here are some key tips:

How to have great conversations

Plan and prepare

Whenever possible it is good to plan and prepare for a great conversation. Doing some preparation beforehand will help us research any information we may need. It will also help us to anticipate and prepare for difficult conversations and any challenges we may need to overcome.

Knowing the purpose of the conversation and what we want to get out of it can be useful in establishing focus. We must, however, ensure that we are not rigid with our plan and keep an open mind, otherwise we may try to dominate the flow of the conversation.

Choose the best timing

It is important to get our timing right especially if we are going to discuss a sensitive issue. We need to think about the other person and what is best for them. This can help us to create a far more suitable setting for the conversation.

If we want to have a positive outcome this can be dependent on getting the timing right. This will enable the listener to be more amenable to our request for a conversation or any feedback we may want to offer.

Be present

The key to a great conversation is to be fully present. Mobile technology can sometimes be extremely distracting for both ourselves and the person we are having the conversation with. Being present and fully engaged is of paramount importance so we must be sure to manage any potential distractions in advance.

Being fully present requires us to make a conscious decision to give the other person our undivided attention. Empathetic people have a way of making us feel as if we are the only person in the room. This is also a sign of respect and can be quite a rarity in today's hyper-distracted digital world.

> Empathy is seeing with the eyes of another, listening with the ears of another, and feeling with the heart of another
>
> Anonymous

Be empathetic

Empathy is our ability to sense other people's emotions and understand how they may be feeling. It is about seeing things from another person's perspective and imagining ourselves in their position. Practising empathy helps us to connect and relate well with other people in our lives.

Humans are social beings, and we all have the capacity to develop empathy which enables us to build stronger and more supportive relationships. By being empathetic we can better "read" another person's inner state and interpret it without blaming, giving advice or attempting to fix the situation.

If you can listen well, people will say you're a good conversationalist

Stanley Bing

Listen actively

Listening is one of the most powerful and constructive ways that we can engage in great conversations. When we practise active listening, we are listening with purpose and with a deep desire to want to really hear what someone else is saying. We will engage in far more fulfilling conversations if we seek to understand the other person's priorities and motivations.

To do this it is important to stay focused and use active listening skills to gain insight. Examples of active listening can be paraphrasing to demonstrate understanding as well as using non-verbal cues such as nodding, eye contact and leaning forward. Brief verbal affirmations can also help to encourage people to be more open and share what is on their mind and how they feel.

> One of the most valuable things we can do to heal one another is listen to each other's stories
>
> Rebecca Falls

Be curious not intrusive

Being curious rather than judgmental about people is a good place to start. A great conversation is the exchange of quality information and often this may be about encouraging detailed explanations. Asking open questions can be very useful. These questions begin with how, why, what, which, when, where and who.

Asking people to describe situations can be a helpful way of enhancing conversations and eliciting more details. It is important to get the balance right however, so that we don't bombard people with too many questions one after the other as that may come across as intrusive.

Challenge assumptions

We all hold unconscious beliefs and biases, and this is triggered by the brain making quick judgments and assessments of people and situations. Often this is influenced by our own background, societal stereotypes and personal experience.

To be a great conversationalist we need to constantly be aware of and challenge our biases about people and stereotyping. Educating ourselves and listening to the groups that are affected by this misinformation is a really important place to start. This is especially important in a world that will thrive through empathy and embracing diversity and inclusivity.

Be assertive

Assertiveness helps us to express ourselves effectively and stand up for what we believe in. It helps us to get our point across while respecting the rights and beliefs of others.

There are 3 ways to build assertiveness:

Be calm – when we are calm, we are more in control. Gentle nostril breathing is a great way to reduce stress and help us feel more relaxed.

Be clear – clarity is so important when we want to get our message understood.

Be confident – we all have a right to an opinion. Not everyone will agree with what we have to say, however that should not diminish our confidence.

Respect silence

How comfortable are you with a pause in a conversation and a moment of silence? In an attempt to be helpful, sometimes we may feel the urge to fill the void and jump in to finish people's sentences, offer them some advice, or even interrupt. Silence can be a very powerful way to simply "be" with another person and give them the space to collect their thoughts and feel calm. This may be especially helpful when the other person is emotional and troubled.

Being comfortable with pauses in conversation and allowing a moment of silence can also communicate acceptance of how the other person may be in that given moment.

Tune into non-verbal communication

Non-verbal communication provides clues to unspoken and underlying concerns and emotions. It can reinforce or contradict what is being said and it is important to remember that communication runs far deeper than words alone.

During a conversation we may observe the other person dodging eye contact, tensing up or shifting about awkwardly. These are important non-verbal signs, and we will then be able to use our powers of empathy by gently asking the other person to describe what is happening for them. This will encourage them to share their feelings openly, knowing that they won't be judged or criticised.

> We all need people who will give us feedback. That's how we improve
>
> Bill Gates

Feedback with evidence

Some conversations may be about providing feedback. This could be perceived as positive or negative depending on how well it is delivered. Feedback in many ways could be considered a gift because it can provide information to either encourage someone to keep doing something or to make useful adjustments and improvements.

It is essential, however, that whenever we offer feedback we provide clear evidence to back up what we are saying and this will add credibility. Another vital ingredient of delivering feedback is to focus on information that will benefit the other person, otherwise it is just pointless criticism.

The single biggest problem in communication is the illusion that it has taken place

George Bernard Shaw

Check for understanding

It is important that we don't just assume that someone else has understood what we are saying, so it is helpful to check for mutual understanding.

The following types of questions can be helpful:

Is what I'm saying clear enough, or is it a bit confusing?

I'm not sure if I'm being clear. What are you hearing?

What is your understanding of what I have just shared with you?

Shall we both recap on what we will take away from the conversation?

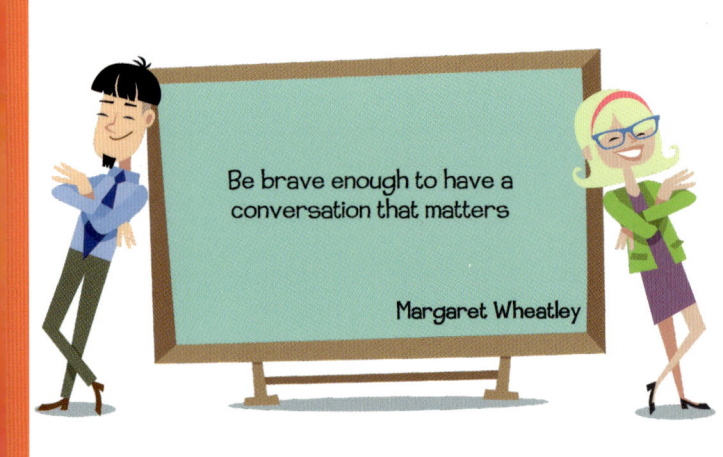

Be brave enough to have a conversation that matters

Margaret Wheatley

Summary

Conversation is such a powerful tool for bringing people together. We live in a wonderfully diverse world where we are connecting with people from so many different backgrounds and we can learn so much from each.

Real-life connections and conversations are important because they provide us with a sense of belonging and support. Great conversations help us to feel better connected to others and to the world around us. So go out into the world today and begin a conversation that matters. You never know what positive impact you could make on someone else's life.

GREAT CONVERSATIONS

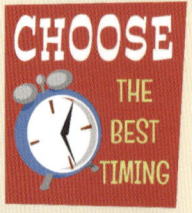

How to communicate well with others

- BE EMPATHETIC
- BE FULLY PRESENT
- BE CURIOUS
- CHALLENGE ASSUMPTIONS
- COMMUNICATE ASSERTIVELY
- CHOOSE THE BEST TIMING
- PROMOTE PSYCHOLOGICAL SAFETY
- CHECK FOR MUTUAL UNDERSTANDING
- Feedback with evidence
- LISTEN ACTIVELY

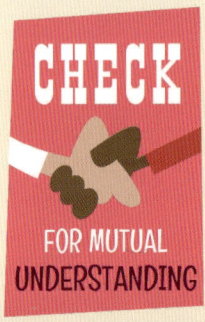

One meaningful conversation can change the course of your life forever

Liggy Webb

Explore more at: www.liggywebb.com